P9-BHT-911

English translation from the Dutch by Clavis Publishing Inc. New York
Copyright © 2018 for the English language edition: Clavis Publishing Inc. New York

Visit us on the web at www.clavisbooks.com

No part of this publication may be reproduced or stored in a retrieval system,
or transmitted in any form or by any means, electronic, mechanical, photocopying,
recording, or otherwise, without the prior written permission of the publisher,
except in the case of brief quotations embodied in critical articles and reviews.
For information regarding permissions, write to Clavis Publishing, info-US@clavisbooks.com

Pilots and What They Do (small size edition) written and illustrated by Liesbet Slegers
Original title: *De piloot*
Translated from the Dutch by Clavis Publishing

ISBN 978-1-60537-383-6

This book was printed in May 2018 at Nikara, M. R. Štefánika 858/25, 963 01 Krupina, Slovenia.

First Edition
10 9 8 7 6 5 4 3 2

Clavis Publishing supports the First Amendment and celebrates the right to read

Pilots
and What They Do
Liesbet Slegers

WITHDRAWN

Clavis

NEW YORK

It's fun to visit a foreign country.
You can get there by car or boat.
But an airplane is even faster!
The pilot will get you there safely.

flying
is fast!

The pilot wears a uniform.
He looks handsome, doesn't he?
The golden stripes on his jacket show his rank.
He has his pilot's hat and pilot's bag.
Both girls and boys can be pilots, of course!

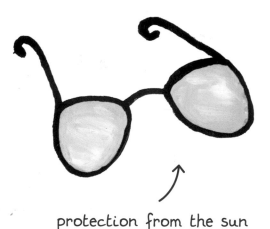

protection from the sun

pilot's hat

tie

pilot's jacket
with stripes

pilot's pants

pilot's bag

The pilot sits in the cockpit,
in the front of the plane.
During the flight, the pilot keeps a close eye
on the instrument panel.
The people in the control tower can see all the
planes on their screens and through the windows.

control column

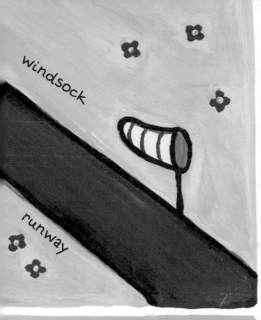

windsock

runway

cockpit

Control tower with
radio contact

Does the airplane have enough fuel?
Is everything ready to go?
The pilot checks everything thoroughly to make
sure the plane and the passengers will be safe!
The luggage is loaded into the cargo hold.

fill 'er up!

The captain is in charge of the airplane
and everyone who works there.
The copilot sits in the cockpit with the captain.
The flight attendants show the passengers how
to travel safely on a plane.
Later, they will bring everyone food and drinks.
Fasten your seatbelts!

yummy!

The pilot is talking to the control tower
over the radio.
They tell him which runway to use.
The engines start and the plane takes the taxiway
to the correct runway.
How exciting!

hello!

The tower tells the pilot he can take off.
Now the brakes are released and the airplane goes
really fast. The pilot pulls the control column and
the nose of the plane goes up. The plane takes off!

flying like
a bird

The plane goes higher and higher,
until it's above the clouds. The pilot checks
everything: height, speed, wind direction....
He gets information during the flight from control
towers of other airports. Is there bad weather
coming? Then we change course.

a storm
ahead?

In the meantime, the pilot can enjoy
the splendid views. The clouds sparkle in the sun.
He can see snow-covered mountains, islands in the
ocean ... Amazing!

what a beautiful
view!

The plane is almost there. The control tower tells the pilot which runway to use.
Slowly, the pilot steers the plane to the ground, pointing the nose down.
The wheels appear again.
Soon the plane touches down on the ground!

← landing gear

The plane has landed. Everyone gets off the plane. The pilots and flight attendants go to a hotel to rest. The captain fills out the paperwork.
Then they get ready to fly to a new destination.

going to a tropical island

Pilots love flying more than anything.
They love feeling as free as a bird.
And you? What do you want to be when you grow up?

let's
fly!

31901064599980